OUR
AMERICA

Growing Up in a New World

in a

New World

1607
to
1775

Brandon Marie Miller

Lerner Publications Company
Minneapolis

This book is lovingly dedicated in memory of my Aunt Jodie and to all the children in our family who grew up long ago in colonial America.

Lerner Publications Company
A division of Lerner Publishing Group
241 First Avenue North
Minneapolis, MN 55401 U.S.A.

Website address: www.lernerbooks.com

Photographs and illustrations in this book are used with the permission of: The Granger Collection, New York, pp. 5, 9, 13, 18 (top), 23, 24, 26, 32, 41, 51, 52; © Stock Montage, Inc., pp. 6, 39, 46 (top), 54, 57, 58; North Wind Picture Archives, pp. 7, 14, 15, 18 (bottom), 20, 25, 29, 37, 45, 49, 50; map illustration by Laura Westlund, pp. 10-11; © Burstein Collection/CORBIS, p. 16; © Bettmann/CORBIS, pp. 17, 28, 53; Brown Brothers, pp. 19, 46 (bottom); © Geoffrey Clements/CORBIS, p. 31; © The Newberry Library/Stock Montage, Inc., pp. 33, 34; © Archivo Iconografo, S.A./CORBIS, p. 42; © Hulton-Deutsch Collection/CORBIS, p. 44.

Front cover image: © Burstein Collection/CORBIS

Library of Congress Cataloging-in-Publication Data

Miller, Brandon Marie.
    Growing Up in a New World, 1607 to 1775 / by Brandon Marie Miller.
        p.   cm. — (Our America)
    Summary: Presents details of daily life of colonial children during the period from 1607 to 1775. Includes bibliographical references and index.
    ISBN: 0–8225–0658–0 (lib. bdg. : alk. paper)
    1. United States—History—Colonial period, ca. 1600–1775—Juvenile literature. 2. United States—Social life and customs—To 1775—Juvenile literature. 3. Children—United States—Social life and customs—17th century—Juvenile literature. 4. Children—United States—Social life and customs—18th century—Juvenile literature. 5. United States—History—Colonial period, ca. 1600–1775—Sources—Juvenile literature. [1. United States—History—Colonial period, ca. 1600–1775. 2. United States—Social life and customs—To 1775.] I. Title. II. Series.
    E188 .M537 2003
    973.2—dc21   2001006826

Manufactured in the United States of America
1 2 3 4 5 6 – JR – 08 07 06 05 04 03

CONTENTS

NOTE TO READERS

Studying history is a way of snooping into the past. To gather clues about a past time, historians study things made during that time. They read old diaries and letters. They look at old newspapers, magazines, advertisements, poems, paintings, and photographs. They listen to old songs. All these things from the past are primary sources.

To write this book, the author used many primary sources. She snooped into life around the time when what we know as the United States was first being settled by Europeans. This time—the colonial period—goes from about 1607 to about 1775.

This lithograph shows the landing of the Pilgrims at Plymouth, Massachusetts, in December 1620. No one at Plymouth made a drawing of this historic moment. This lithograph was made years later, in 1876.

Many books about this period are historical fiction. Historical fiction is a made-up story that is set in a real time. In this book, the people you will meet are real. You'll discover paintings and drawings of them. You'll find quotes from their diaries and letters. You'll notice many things that are different from modern times. For example, people of this era spelled words quite differently. Their words are printed here just the way they wrote them.

By studying all these primary sources, you'll have a chance to do some snooping of your own. Your ideas about the past can help all of us build a better understanding of it.

CHAPTER ONE

HOWLING WILDERNESS to PLEASANT LAND

Rise up, my children, time is ripe!
Old things are passed away....
A little ship have I prepared
To bear you o'er the seas.

—*poet Jeremiah Eames Rankin, 1620*

* *

'Tis a bleak, cold December in 1620. After three months aboard a ship called the *Mayflower*, the passengers are finally viewing their "wetherbeaten" new home on the coast of Massachusetts. A handful of colonists had already settled at Jamestown, Virginia, in 1607. The first arrivals at that colony had all been men. But the *Mayflower*'s 102 passengers include women and 31 children. The youngest child is an infant. Born on the voyage, little Oceanus was named for the great ocean all around.

After the *Mayflower* has arrived in the New World of North America, its passengers cannot easily return home to Europe. The Atlantic Ocean swells as a giant barrier between them and "all the civill parts of the world," as *Mayflower* leader William Bradford put it.

Opposite: Passengers from the *Mayflower* row to the Massachusetts shore. *Right*: Among the *Mayflower*'s passengers were thirty-one children.

On Board the *Mayflower*

The *Mayflower* passengers faced crowded, cramped conditions during their journey across the ocean. The ship leaked, leaving them wet and shivering in their quarters belowdecks. Most often dinner was just a bit of salted beef and hard, dry biscuits washed down with beer. Children passed the long hours by playing games such as cat's cradle and find-the -slipper. Only in good weather could children run free in the fresh air on the ship's deck.

One boy, fourteen-year-old Francis Billington, was considered a troublemaker. He once fired a musket (a kind of gun) inside the *Mayflower*. Sparks from the blast ignited a fire. The flames almost spread to barrels storing explosive gunpowder. The *Mayflower* passengers were furious. Leader William Bradford wondered how Francis and the rest of his "profane" (evil) family had "shuffled into our company."

Among the children are Ellen More, age eight, Jasper More, age seven, Richard More, age six, and Mary More, age four. They huddle together, wondering what awaits them. Their father, Samuel More, had taken them from their mother after a bitter divorce battle. He had placed them on board the *Mayflower* in England. He had paid for their passage (the cost of their trip) and arranged for each child to receive fifty acres of land in the New World. Then he had said good-bye. Little Ellen, Jasper, Richard, and Mary are facing this test of survival alone.

The First Winter

In Europe cities bustled with crowded markets, taverns, and shops. The towering stone churches there were already hundreds of years old. In the New World, however, no churches and no houses with warm firesides welcomed the travelers. No taverns offered ale to quench their thirst. No shops sold bread.

Instead, trees crowded darkly against the winter sky. Brambles and broken branches littered the forest floor. The only roads were faint footpaths used by Native Americans winding through the woods. The shadowy forest and haunting silence made many of the European travelers uneasy. So did the tales they had heard back home about the "savage" Indians living in the New World.

Women and children lived on board the *Mayflower* at first. The men hauled supplies ashore and began building shelters for the new settlement, named Plymouth. When winter arrived, the "sharp and violent" weather caught everyone unprepared. Weakened by the voyage, the settlers quickly began falling ill. At one point, only six or seven people were healthy enough to care for the sick.

Colonists struggled to build shelters during the first winter at Plymouth (which they spelled Plimoth).

People began dying. Two thirteen-year-old girls, Mary Chilton and Elizabeth Tilley, lost both their parents. Sixteen-year-old Priscilla Mullins lost her mother, father, and brother Joseph. Baby Samuel Eaton was left motherless. The three Allerton children, ages eight, six, and four, lost their mother and their baby brother. Three of the abandoned More children died. Only six-year-old Richard survived.

By March fifty *Mayflower* passengers lay buried in New World graves. Ten children had died. Ten had lost at least one parent. And four had lost their guardians. The remaining families gathered orphaned children into their care.

* * * *

PLANTING COLONIES

Despite the hardships, thousands of "new-comers" sailed to America each year. England, Spain, France, Holland, and other nations all rushed their citizens to the New World. Once settled, colonists could supply their mother country in Europe with a stream of goods—gold, fur, timber, and foods. Colonies increased not only a European nation's wealth but also its power and glory.

Becoming a colonist was a grim and dangerous business. Why did so many people agree to sail to America? Many dreamed of riches and adventure. Others hoped to find religious freedom. About half the *Mayflower* passengers sailed for this reason. Later these immigrants were called Pilgrims.

English Puritans flocked to Massachusetts Bay Colony, founded in 1630. They wanted a church more "pure" than the one they had left in England. The church was so important to them that it governed the colony.

Gradually England came to control much of the eastern coast of North America. By 1733 it had thirteen well-established colonies there.

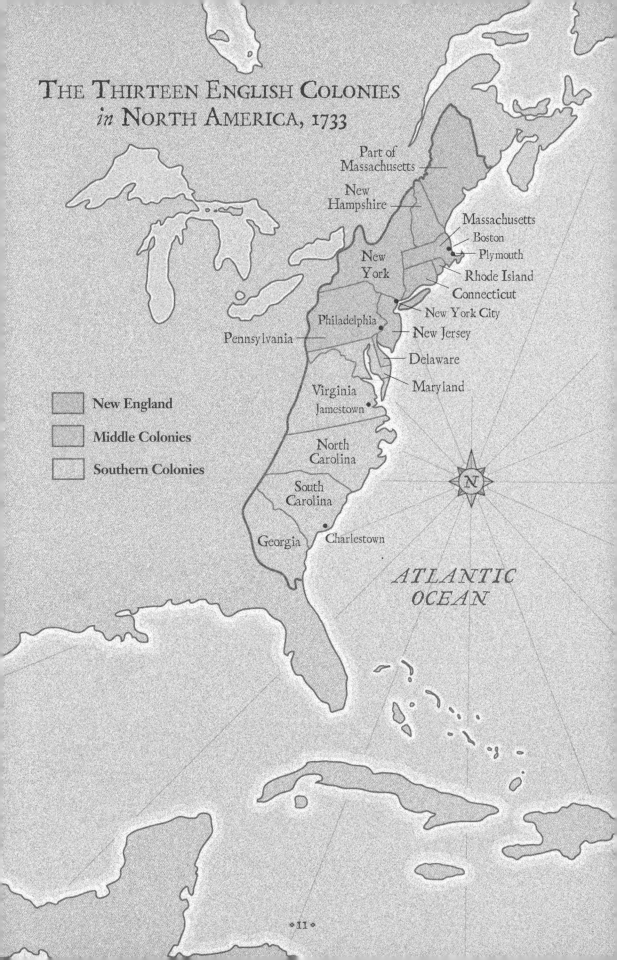

THE THIRTEEN ENGLISH COLONIES
in NORTH AMERICA, 1733

Part of Massachusetts

New Hampshire

Massachusetts
Boston
Plymouth
Rhode Island
Connecticut
New York City

New York

Philadelphia
New Jersey

Pennsylvania

Delaware

Maryland

Virginia
Jamestown

North Carolina

South Carolina

Georgia
Charlestown

New England

Middle Colonies

Southern Colonies

N

ATLANTIC OCEAN

Weary, Weary, Weary

The colonies were a place of never-ending, exhausting work—and too few workers. Some people, known as indentured servants, had agreed to work for a master. In return, indentured servants received their passage to the New World. Indentured servants often labored for fifteen hours a day under harsh conditions. When their time of service ended (after about four to seven years), they were free to marry and to build a free life.

To help pay a family's passage to America, some parents indentured their children. "Many parents, to pay their fares . . . have to barter away their children as if they were cattle. . . , " wrote one German man. "Since the fathers and mothers often do not know where their children's masters live, or even who they are, it often happens that parents and children do not see each other again for many years, sometimes never." A child's indenture usually lasted until his or her eighteenth or twenty-first birthday.

> "It often happens that parents and children do not see each other again for many years, sometimes never."
> —Gottlieb Mittleberger, 1750s

A Humble New Home

Many of the earliest houses in the colonies were quickly built from wood and dried clay. Most had just one room with a large fireplace for cooking. The only floor was the ground. A few tiny windows dimly lit the room. People didn't have glass, so they covered the windows with oiled cloth. A wooden ladder led to an overhead loft stuffed with supplies. Children climbed up to sleep beside barrels of salted fish and cloth sacks filled with cornmeal or dried peas.

Colonists attacked the New World's vast forests, clearing land for villages and farms with axes and fire. In New England—Massachusetts and the surrounding region—the soil was rocky. Farms there were often small. In the South, farms were larger. A few southern farms grew into huge plantations with thousands of acres. These plantations were like mini-towns, fueled by the labor of slaves. By age ten, a slave child worked like an adult, larboring long days in the fields.

The colonial frontier crept steadily westward as people followed rivers inland from the sea. Colonists widened paths and tramped

TAKEN BY FORCE

In 1619 (one year before the *Mayflower* arrived), a Dutch ship captain sold twenty captured Africans (*right*) to Virginia colonists. In the following years, thousands of Africans were kidnapped, crammed into ships, and taken to the colonies. Many were children and teenagers. Those who survived the journey were then sold. Many of the first Africans to arrive worked for a set period of time, like indentured servants. But by the late 1600s, colonial governments passed separate laws for African workers. The laws sentenced most African Americans in the colonies—and their children—to a lifetime of slavery.

new dirt roads, usually with nothing but their own two legs for transportation.

The European invasion was devastating to Native American families. Thousands died from diseases such as smallpox that were carried by Europeans. Colonists' pigs and cows often roamed free, trampling native fields. In addition, settlers and native tribes often fought with each other. Europeans burned native villages and killed or captured many Native Americans. Many tribes survived by moving west, away from the colonists.

Many Native Americans died from diseases they caught from colonists.

* * * *

SETTLING IN FOR GOOD

By the time the American Revolution began in 1775, more than 2.5 million people called the colonies home. About half a million of them were African Americans. Most people lived on farms. Others lived in large towns such as Boston, Massachusetts; New York City, New York; Philadelphia, Pennsylvania; and Charleston, South Carolina.

By the 1660s, Boston, Massachusetts, was a thriving seaport town. A youngster could buy rock candy and other treats in its many bustling shops.

Farm families grew what they needed—vegetables, fruits, and grains. They raised sheep and other animals. Even town dwellers picked vegetables from backyard gardens and raised chickens or pigs. In the largest towns, a youngster could buy a tin whistle or rock candy at one of many shops, slide into the boys' or girls' pew in church on Sunday, or even watch live actors perform a play.

Over the years, families improved their homes. They covered dirt floors with wooden planks. They added rooms. Some even ordered gleaming glass windows from Europe. The wealthiest colonists built elegant homes of ten rooms or more.

By the 1770s, times were different from the dark, early months at Plymouth. A "howling wilderness" had been transformed into a "Pleasant land." At home, generations of colonial youngsters struggled to grow from howling infants into pleasant and dutiful children.

YOUR DUTIFUL CHILD

❋ ❋

In the frosty darkness of a February morning in 1700, a newborn baby cries at the Smith house. A midwife has just helped the mother deliver the baby. She carries the child to the fireplace, where she warms his tiny body. Next she folds a square of diaper cloth around the baby's bottom. She fastens it with straight pins.

Then the midwife rubs the baby's bent arms and legs. She carefully pulls them straight. She wraps narrow strips of cloth called swaddling around his straightened body. She's glad to see that the swaddling binds him tightly, like a mummy. This child must not grow crooked.

Opposite: In this 1671 portrait, six-month-old Mary Freake is probably wearing stays (underclothes that keep her stiff and straight). *Above*: A colonial woman gives birth.

❋ ❋ ❋ ❋

WELCOME LITTLE STRANGER

On that wintry morning, the baby's family did not welcome a tiny human being. They thought of the baby as a "lump of flesh," a "round ball" who had to be stretched and molded into a human.

This illustration, made after the colonial period, shows two colonial youngsters minding themselves while adults churn butter, spin thread, cook at the fire, peel vegetables, and roll dough.

Humans talked, thought, and believed in God. Babies—like animals—did none of these things. Instead, they soiled their clothing, slobbered, and howled like little beasts.

Colonial parents feared babies might never stand straight and walk like humans. Instead, babies might crawl like animals all their lives. So families pushed babies to walk early. Walking showed that a child was on the right path to becoming a full human being.

Baby Smith joined a large family (many families in the 1600s and 1700s had ten or more children). The baby's mother was busy with her other children and with many chores. As long as the baby seemed safe, she mostly ignored him. She unwrapped him only a few times a day to pin

Peregrine White, a boy born at Plymouth, slept in a wicker cradle like this one.

on a fresh diaper. Then she wound him back into a swaddled package.

Mostly, colonial parents gave their small children little extra care. They seldom rushed to pick up a crying baby. They believed babies cried to exercise their lungs. Or maybe babies cried for selfish reasons, and that had to stop!

Baby Smith stayed in swaddling clothes for about three or four months. He lay in a narrow cradle while his family bustled around him. Like other tiny children in early America, he had to fit into the rest of his family as best he could.

* * * *

STANDING STOOLS AND PUDDING CAPS

Once out of swaddling, baby girls and boys wore loose dresses longer than their legs. Thankfully, the long skirts made crawling difficult. No parent wished to see their child crawling!

Many busy mothers stuck their babies into a handy standing stool (a short stool with a hole in the seat). It held babies about the waist while their little legs dangled above the floor. Some babies endured hour after miserable hour this way. But at least a standing stool kept a child safe from falling into the fireplace or down the stairs. Some parents encouraged walking with a go-cart, a standing stool with wheels.

When little ones began to walk, they wore shorter, ankle-length dresses. Parents often strapped a

Robert Gibbs is age four in this 1670 painting. Toddler boys wore dresses until about age five.

padded cap called a pudding cap onto their toddler's head. The cap protected the child from bumps, which people believed turned the brain soft like pudding. No one wanted a child to become a stupid "pudding head."

Toddlers—and even tiny babies—sometimes wore stays under their clothes. Stays wrapped stiffly around a child's middle, helping to keep the child straight.

* * * *

ALL HANDS ARE NEEDED

Survival in the colonies depended on hard work. Even the smallest hands pitched in. Three-year-olds planted seeds in the kitchen garden near the house. They pulled weeds and chased birds away from the young plants. They gathered twigs for kindling fires.

Older children swept floors with brooms they made themselves. They hauled water, milked cows, and gathered eggs.

Both boys and girls carded and combed thick sheep's wool, then spun it into thread for weaving and knitting. Children also stuffed sausages, dipped candles, and stirred batches of soap. A Connecticut

Both boys and girls did chores on colonial farms.

A Lesson in Honesty

Benjamin Franklin wrote the story of his life in an autobiography. Writing about his childhood, he remembered, "I was generally a leader among the boys, and sometimes led them into scrapes [trouble]."

Once Ben and his friends wished they had a wharf "fit for us to stand upon" at their favorite fishing spot. Ben led his friends to a nearby construction site and showed them "a large heap of stones, which were intended for a new house." After the builders left, the boys went back for the stones and "brought them all away and built our little wharff." The theft was soon noticed, and the thieves were caught. "Several of us were corrected by our fathers," Ben wrote. In colonial times, being corrected usually meant getting a whipping or a spanking. Ben later wrote that his father "convinced me that nothing was useful which was not honest."

boy remembered "bringing in fuel for the day, cutting potatoes for the sheep, feeding the swine, watering the horses, picking berries, gathering the vegetables, spooling the yarn."

Children's work trained them for their roles as adults. Like other girls, the daughters of the famous minister Cotton Mather were expected to become housewives. They needed to know how to cook, of course. Since doctors were scarce, they also needed to know how to tend the sick. "To accomplish my little daughters for housekeeping," Mather wrote in 1710, "I . . . have them, at least once a week, to prepare some new thing, either for diet or medicine."

Under a mother's guidance, a girl learned to mend and sew, churn butter, and brew beer. Daughters helped salt, smoke, and pickle meats, fruits, and vegetables for eating in winter, when fresh food was scarce. They learned how to run a thrifty house, never wasting a penny.

Boys helped their fathers. They hunted, fished, and chopped wood for cooking and heating. Farm boys grew strong swinging the sharp blade of a scythe to cut wheat, oats, and barley. In towns, sons worked at trades alongside their fathers. Tradesmen provided goods and services to others. The son of a carpenter helped build furniture. The son of a cooper helped make barrels.

Benjamin Franklin, a future leader in the American Revolution, was ten when he began working in his father's shop in Boston. He helped make candles and soap. "I was employed in cutting Wick for the Candles," Ben later wrote, "filling the dipping Mold, . . . attending the Shop, [and] going on errands."

* * * *

STUBBORNNESS AND PRIDE

Colonial parents believed children had a "stubbernes and stoutnes of minde arising from naturall pride." This pride needed to be "broken and beaten down." A stubborn, prideful youngster was often whipped or spanked.

Colonial children listened to endless home lessons on honesty and honor. Ideally, daughters also learned modesty and silence. When Jane Coleman was ten, in 1718, her father advised her, "My dear child, . . . I charge you. . . . fear to sin. Be very dutiful to your Mother, and respectful to everybody. Be very humble and modest, womanly and discreet."

Disobedient youngsters were punished severely. In New Jersey and Connecticut, a child over age sixteen could be put to death "without mercy" for hitting or cursing a parent.

> *"I charge you. . . . Be very dutiful to your Mother, and respectful to everybody. Be very humble and modest, womanly and discreet."*
> —*Jane Coleman's father, 1718*

RESPECT ADULTS!

Youngsters were expected to obey their parents and leaders such as the king of England, who ruled the American colonies. By studying *The New-England Primer* (right), a schoolbook, thousands of children learned to chant: "I Will fear GOD, and honour the KING. I will honour my Father & Mother. I will Obey my Superiours. I will Submit to my Elders."

Now the Child being entred in his Letters and Spelling, let him learn these and such like Sentences by Heart, whereby he will be both instructed in his Duty, and encouraged in his Learning.

The Dutiful Child's Promises.

I Will fear GOD, and honour the KING.
I will honour my Father & Mother.
I will Obey my Superiours.
I will Submit to my Elders.
I will Love my Friends.
I will hate no Man.
I will forgive my Enemies, and pray to God for them.
I will as much as in me lies keep all God's Holy Commandments.

When Elizabeth Sprigs disobeyed her father, he banished her from home. She had to become an indentured servant. Her master whipped her and abused her with angry words. Finally Elizabeth wrote her father a tear-stained letter, describing her life. She slept on the ground, she said. She had only "Indian corn and salt to eat, and that even begrudged." Elizabeth begged her father to send her some clothes, since she was "almost naked, no shoes nor stockings." She signed the letter, "Your undutiful and disobedient child, Elizabeth Sprigs, September 22, 1756."

CHAPTER THREE

FOOLING
the
OLD
DELUDER

"Satan finds some Mischief still

Most families in colonial America believed a struggle between God and the Devil (the "Old Deluder") surrounded their lives. The Devil tried to get them to sin. If people fought against sin, God might help them prosper. If they gave in to sin, disaster would follow.

No one carried these beliefs further than the Puritans of New England. Their rules for obeying God were strict. For example, no Puritan adult worked on the Sabbath (Sunday). No child played. Even cooking was forbidden.

Puritan families spent the Sabbath in church, praying and reviewing their faults. Sermons lasted for hours. Officials watched for people snoozing in the pews. Children were told, "Fix thine eye upon the Minister; Let it not wildly wander to gaze upon any Person or Thing." After services, youngsters should not race from the church "as if thou wert weary of being there."

Raising a flock of ignorant, idle children was a Puritan's worst nightmare. The best way for children to escape the Old Deluder was to study the Bible. When Cotton Mather's son Samuel was six, the Reverend Mather gave him a Bible verse to memorize. "My proposal," noted Sammy's father, "was to have the child improve in

Opposite: Puritan families in church. *Above*: A drawing of New England's first church. Religion influenced almost every detail of life for Puritan youngsters.

for idle hands to do." —*from a poem by Isaac Watts, 1715*

goodness at the same time, that he improved in reading."

In 1647 Massachusetts passed a law to help make sure everyone could read the Bible. The law required towns with more than fifty families to keep a school and hire a teacher. All children—boys and girls, rich and poor—could attend. Math and writing were less important in these schools than reading the word of God.

* * * * *

AN ABUSE OF PRECIOUS TIME

Colonial children were seldom allowed to be idle. Time was a gift from God. Wasting time was sinful. A children's song from the early 1700s reminded young people to be useful. "Satan finds some mischief . . . , " said the song, "for idle hands to do."

A Boston judge was horrified by one boy's waste of time. On April 1, 1708, the judge saw a six-year-old call to a stranger that the stranger's shoes were not tied. When the stranger stopped and looked down at his shoes, the child cried, "April Fool!" The judge later fumed in a letter he wrote, "What an abuse is it of precious time!"

Severall young men playing at foote-ball on the Ice upon the Lords-Day are all Drownd

This engraving from *Divine Examples of God's Severe Judgements upon Sabbath-Breakers* shows Puritan boys drowning because they played football on the Sabbath.

AGAINST IDLENESS AND MISCHIEF

How doth the little busy Bee
Improve each shining Hour,
And gather Honey all the day
From every opening Flower!...

In Works of Labour or of Skill
I would be busy too:
For *Satan* finds some Mischief still
For idle Hands to do.

—*Isaac Watts, 1715*

"NO SOONER COME, BUT GONE"

Danger lurked around every corner for colonial children. Some youngsters drowned in wells. Others fell into rivers or broke through the thin ice glazing winter ponds. A child could be run over by horses or a farm wagon or bitten by a poisonous snake. Children suffered burns from tripping into fireplaces. And almost all homes had guns (for hunting and for protection), which caused many deadly accidents.

Sickness was also a constant enemy. People had no refrigerators, so food often spoiled. Rotten food caused stomach cramps and diarrhea. Epidemic diseases stalked from family to family and from town to town. Smallpox, diphtheria, whooping cough, and measles sickened many children and killed thousands.

Colonial doctors knew little about the human body and disease. They knew nothing about bacteria and viruses. So they had few weapons with which to fight illness. To cure a fever, a doctor bled

This painting shows a woman being bled into a bowl.

his patient. This meant opening a vein and letting the patient's blood run into a "bleeding bowl." Doctors often brewed medicines from plants and minerals. Some medicines purged patients "Upward and Downward" (which meant the medicine caused vomiting and bowel movements). Most families just doctored themselves. They concocted their own medicines using everything from tree bark to sheep's dung.

With so many illnesses and so few remedies, death spared few families. As many as half of all children died before the age of nine. The Reverend Cotton Mather outlived all but two of his sixteen children.

MORE ABOUT BLEEDING

Thomas Palmer was a New England doctor in the 1690s. Here is part of his treatment for a child suffering from a sore throat.

"The cure is by purging downwards & bleeding…by pricking the inflamed parts of the throat by a Lancet a small knife tyed to a flat stick, by bleeding under the tongue, in one of the Veins or both, houlding warm water in the mouth while the patient bleedeth."

"WHAT SHALL I WISH TO HAVE DONE?"

Puritans believed that all people were born sinful. Children needed to struggle against sin so that they wouldn't go to hell if they died. To help them remember this, many colonial schoolchildren memorized this verse: "I in the Burying Place may see / Graves shorter there than I / From Death's Arrest no Age is free / Young Children too may die."

Cotton Mather believed all children should ask, "What shall I wish to have done if I were now a-dying?" One evening Mather invited his four-year-old daughter Katy into his study. He told Katy that she must struggle to be good because of "the sinful Condition of her Nature." Then he advised Katy to "pray . . . every Day. That God . . . would give her a New Heart."

Such lessons could be frightening. In 1689 the father of an eleven-year-old Boston boy named Samuel heard about another youngster's death. He advised Samuel "to prepare for death, and therefore to . . . really pray." Samuel "burst out into a bitter cry . . . afraid he should die," wrote the father in his diary. The two of them prayed together "and read scriptures comforting against death."

Cotton Mather in a fashionable wig

> *"I have not been thankful and humble as I should have been. Therefore God is righteous in afflicting me."*
>
> —the Rev. Increase Mather, 1675

Some people believed God might punish sinful parents by taking a child's life. When one minister's two sons lay ill in 1675, he wrote, "I have not been thankful and humble as I should have been. Therefore God is righteous in afflicting me." Both sons recovered.

STEPFAMILIES STEP IN

Sometimes parents also died young. Mothers faced an especially dangerous time during childbirth. Many mothers and fathers tried to plan for their deaths. Many parents named uncles or older brothers as guardians of young children. Wealthy parents left money or property to support their youngsters.

Even when grieving the death of a husband or wife, adults were practical. Husbands and wives needed each other as work partners. Women worked mainly within the home and raised the children. Men worked in businesses or on farms. Since two parents were necessary for a family's survival, most parents remarried within a few months after the death of a spouse. Susanna White, the mother of two small children, remarried at Plymouth, Massachusetts, in May 1621, just three months after her husband died. Mrs. White married Edward Winslow, whose wife had also died only months before.

In fact, parents might marry two or three times during their lives. Cotton Mather married three times.

Given all these deaths and remarriages, children could end up living in a stepfamily with no blood relatives of their own. Anne

Bradstreet, a colonial mother and poet, worried about this when she was expecting a baby. She wrote a poem begging her husband to choose a stepdame (a stepmother) carefully if she died. "Look to my little babes," she wrote. "These O protect from step-dame's injury."

According to Bradstreet's poem, the "wicked step-mother" found in fairy tales might have been a real concern in the 1600s. The most famous wicked stepmother appeared in Charles Perrault's version of *Cinderella*, published in France in 1697. A stepdame might have little interest in her new husband's offspring. She might favor her own children and neglect her stepchildren, or send them away to work.

Mothers and fathers in colonial America loved their children. They dreaded being separated from them by death, which seemed to be always waiting on their doorsteps. Cotton Mather deeply mourned the death of his two-year-old daughter in 1711. "I am called unto the sacrifice of my dear, dear daughter Jerusha," he wrote. "I begged, I begged, that such a bitter cup, as the death of that lovely child, might pass from me." No wonder parents hurried their youngsters into adulthood. Childhood was no place to linger.

A painting by Ralph Earl, late 1700s, of Mrs. Noah Smith and her children. Colonial parents had large families and loved their children, just as modern parents do.

CHAPTER FOUR

LEARNING PRETTY FAST

"*Labor for learning before you grow old*

On a January day in 1691, a group of boys, and a few girls, sit on benches in the "common school" in a Massachusetts town. They range in age from five-year-olds to teens. The school has one room, which is dimly lit and freezing cold. Students who supplied firewood sit near the flames, toasty warm. Those who forgot sit in the back, huddled in coats and cradling their inkwells in stiff hands to thaw the ink.

The students work busily under the sharp eye of the schoolmaster, their teacher. Like most teachers in colonial times, he is a man. Students learn by copying (rewriting) or memorizing lessons they repeat after the schoolmaster. No one asks questions. Few schoolmasters encourage questions or free thinking!

Older students scratch math sums onto birch-bark paper with quill pens. The youngest chant their letters from *The New-England Primer*: "*A*, In *Adam's* Fall We Sinned all. *B*, Thy Life to Mend This *Book* Attend." When the children get to *F*, a few eyes glance at the birch switch on the schoolmaster's desk. "*F*, The Idle *Fool* Is whipt at School."

Younger children begin lessons at home with a parent for a teacher. Some go to a neighbor woman's house for lessons. In these schools,

A In *Adam's* Fall
We Sinned all.

B Thy Life to Mend
This *Book* Attend.

C The *Cat* doth play
And after slay.

D A *Dog* will bite
A Thief at night.

E An *Eagles* flight
Is out of sight.

F The Idle *Fool*
Is whipt at School.

Opposite: A dame school. *Right*: A page from *The New-England Primer*, 1727

for it is better than silver or gold."

—*words stitched on a sampler by a young girl, 1736*

called dame schools, the "dame" is usually an older widow earning extra money teaching youngsters. She spins wool, knits, or cooks while listening to her students recite.

Young students learn the alphabet and simple poems from a hornbook. A hornbook is a wooden paddle with a printed page attached to it. To protect the page, the paddle is covered with a thin layer of animal horn. The horn is so thin you can read through it.

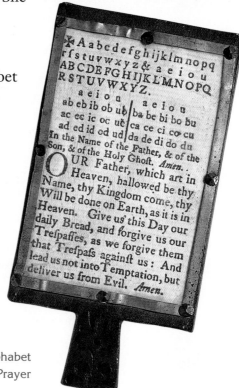

A hornbook, showing the alphabet and the Lord's Prayer

* * * *

"SUCH THINGS AS BELONG TO WOMEN"

In colonial times, more boys than girls attended school. Boys also attended school longer than girls. After common school, boys had several choices. Some continued their education at a Latin grammar school. A few went on to college. Many left education behind and learned a trade or worked on the family farm.

A girl might be taught to read and write. But once she had mastered a bit of each, her formal education usually ended. A daughter's real training came at home. An accomplished woman was a successful wife, mother, and homemaker. Most people in colonial America thought education was a waste of time for a girl. Many feared an educated woman might stick her nose into male arenas—politics, business, and religion. One of Anne Bradstreet's poems claimed people found her writing "obnoxious." They thought that into her hand "a sewing needle better fits" instead of "a poet's pen."

Besides, people believed a girl's body and brain couldn't cope with the stresses of learning. In 1645 John Winthrop, the first governor of Massachusetts Bay Colony, described a woman who "lost her understanding and reason" by "giving herself wholly to reading and writing." Such things were only "proper for men, whose minds are stronger." The woman's insanity could have been avoided, claimed the governor, "if she had attended her household affairs and such things as belong to women."

> *One woman "lost her understanding and reason" by "giving herself wholly to reading and writing."*
>
> —*John Winthrop, governor of Massachussetts Bay Colony, 1645*

* * * *

"DOWN TO BOOK"

Only daughters of wealthy families got a chance to further their education. Men with money hired private tutors for their sons, and sometimes daughters shared lessons. A tutor lived in the family's spacious home. School often lasted all day. One girl complained of the long hours:

> *Up I get, huddle on my cloaths & down to Book, then to Breakfast, then to School again, & may be I have an Hour to my self before Dinner, then the Same Story over again til twilight, & then a small portion of time before I go to rest.*

Eliza Lucas of South Carolina loved to study. She was especially interested in the "vegetable world" (meaning plants and farming).

"You Write Better Already"

Betty Pratt's brother was going to school in England in 1732. Eleven-year-old Betty wrote to him, "I find you have got the start of me in learning very much, for you write better already than I can expect to do as long as I live." Betty also told him, "I can't cast up a sum in addition clearly, but I am striving to do better everyday. I can perform a great many dances." She was also learning to sew. But, she confessed, "I cannot speak a word of French."

As a teenager in the 1730s, Eliza managed three plantations for her father. She devoted about five years to experiments with the indigo plant (the plant used for making blue dyes). Eliza passed seeds along to her neighbors and eventually introduced indigo to the whole colony. It became a major "cash crop" that could be sold for profit.

But harder subjects such as biology, business, and math were usually skipped for young ladies. Instead, girls concentrated on social skills: dancing, singing, and perhaps learning French.

Benjamin Franklin thought girls needed math and business skills. If a woman's husband died and left her with a family to care for, these skills would help her more "than either Music or Dancing," argued Franklin. An educated mother could keep the family business running until "a Son is grown up fit to . . . go on with it."

African American Children at School

Almost all slave children were forbidden to go to school. Instead, they learned adult jobs by working alongside adults. Most young slaves worked in the fields. Others learned skills such as carpentry, weaving, or cooking.

Phillis Wheatley was an accomplished writer. But the lettering on this 1773 portrait calls her only the "Negro Servant" of Mr. John Wheatley.

Phillis Wheatley was one of a very few African American children to receive an education. Born in Africa in about 1753, Phillis was captured and taken to Boston. The family who bought Phillis taught her to read and write. Phillis wrote essays and poetry and became the first published African American writer.

Eliza Lucas of South Carolina was a slave owner who taught a few slave children how to read. "I intend [them to become] school mistres's for the rest of the Negroe children," she explained. The people of Williamsburg, Virginia, opened a special school for slave children in 1760. The children in this school learned to read the Bible. But they rarely continued their education much longer. They were put to work instead.

. . . .

NO SCHOOLMASTER FOR FOUR YEARS

Some colonial children never went to school. Others learned to read a bit, but they could not write. They signed their names with an *X*, called their mark. In 1662 one Virginia man complained about "this want of schooles." He said Virginia's lack of schools made "children born in Virginia . . . unserviceable for any government Employments either in Church or State."

At the age of fifteen, Miss Mary Ball of Virginia wrote to a friend. "We have not had a schoolmaster in our neighborhood . . . in nearly four years," she said. Mary (the future mother of George Washington) lived on a farm. Children on farms had less chance for an education than children in towns. Any book learning came from their parents—if their parents could read or write, that is.

Mary Ball's family finally hired a teacher. "We have now a young minister living with us. . . . He teaches school for his board," she wrote. "He teaches Sister Susie and me and Madam Carter's boy and two girls. I am now learning pretty fast."

In rural areas, several families might join together to hire a schoolmaster. They often built a schoolhouse in one of the families' fields. To reach a "field school," neighboring children traveled several miles by riding horseback, walking, or even rowing a boat.

George Washington attended a Virginia field school for a few

GOODY TWOSHOES

Goodness was rewarded in many books that colonial children read. One popular book was *The History of Little Goody Twoshoes*. It tells the tale of Margery Twoshoes, an orphan who grows up to be a wise and good schoolmistress. Margery went from "Rags and Care, and having shoes but half a Pair" to riding in a fine coach pulled by six horses—wealth indeed! Samuel Richardson's popular novel *Pamela* (1740) tells the story of a servant girl whose goodness and modesty wins her master's love.

George Washington had little formal education. As a young man, he learned surveying skills.

years, off and on. His formal education ended by age thirteen. Like other colonists, Washington gained much of his knowledge by reading on his own. So did Benjamin Franklin, whose formal schooling ended by age ten.

Education often ended early because many people believed learning a trade was more important. Whether rich or poor, anyone with a skill could always be sure of earning a living. William Penn, the founder of Pennsylvania, put it this way. "The poor may work to live, and the rich, if they become poor, may not want." Some wealthy people thought education would make poor children rebellious. "I thank God, we have not free schools . . . , " wrote the governor of Virginia in 1671, "for learning has brought disobedience into the world."

* * * *

RULES OF CIVILITY

When a horseback rider wearing a fine coat and a wig trotted toward young Devereaux Jarrett in 1740, Jarrett froze. A wig was "a badge of gentle folk." This was a gentleman! Jarrett darted into a shop doorway and waited while the man passed. "We were accustomed to look upon . . . gentle folks, as beings of a superior

Sleep Not
When Others Speak

Around 1746 fourteen-year-old George Washington sat down with an English book of manners and copied out 110 rules he wanted to follow. He wanted not only to become a better person but also to gain a good position in society. George later grew up to become the first president of the United States. Here are some of his "rules of civility."

Sleep not when others speak, sit not when others stand.

In speaking to men of quality, do not lean nor look them full in the face, nor approach too near them, at least keep a full pace from them.

Run not in the streets; neither go too slowly nor with mouth open.

When eating, scratch not; neither spit, cough, or blow your nose, except if there is a necessity for it.

Labour to keep alive in your heart that little heavenly fire called conscience.

—from George Washington's *Rules of Civility & Decent Behavior in Company and Conversation*

Young George Washington tips his hat to a gentleman wearing a wig.

order . . . ," Jarrett later wrote. "I was quite shy of them, and kept off at a humble distance."

Like fine clothes, good manners were also a sign of social status. People "of quality" drilled their children in proper etiquette. Rude people were "lower class." As a son in one rich Virginia family wrote, "Better be never born than ill-bred."

Some of the most popular books in colonial America were books listing rules for good manners. "Never sit in the presence of thy Parents without bidding," one rulebook advised dutiful children. "Dispute not, nor delay to do thy Parents Commands."

> *"Dispute not, nor delay to do thy Parents Commands."*
> —*Colonial manners book*

CHAPTER FIVE

RECREATIONS

"I spent my time ... in driving hoops, playing marbles ... wrestling, swimming, skating."

—U. S. president John Adams, writing about his boyhood in the 1730s

Colonists usually spared little time for merrymaking and leisure. In England, fairs, festivals, and feasting were part of village life. But most colonists lived on scattered farms, miles from a village or town. They got together for celebrations less often.

Unlike people in modern times, colonists had no quick means to hear news. Few newspapers existed. Mail took weeks, maybe even months, to reach people. Starved for news of the outside world, colonists often welcomed travelers into their homes. In 1702 a European visitor praised Virginia hospitality. Everywhere he went, rich and poor alike offered him free food and lodging. "It is possible," he wrote, "to travel through the whole country without money." Some visits lasted for weeks.

> *"It is possible to travel through the whole country without money."*
>
> —*Francis Louis Michel, 1702*

HOLIDAYS

As good English people, colonists did celebrate births and marriages in the English royal family. Throughout the year, each colony set aside days of thanksgiving for fasting and prayer.

Election Days beckoned people to town, creating an air of celebration. So did Court Days, when the court heard cases and complaints. Members of the colony's militia (army) gathered during Training Days. Training Days often turned rowdy as men guzzled too many tankards of rum and ale. New England ministers complained the men came to "smoke, carouse, and swagger, and dishonour God." Men and boys sometimes trudged home bruised from wrestling matches held during Training Days.

A rowdy Guy Fawkes Day celebration in London, England, in the 1600s

A traditional English holiday was Guy Fawkes Day. Held on November 5, the day celebrated the end of a plot by Guy Fawkes to blow up the English king and the Parliament building (where the English government works). In the colonies, young men used Guy Fawkes Day as an excuse to roam the streets lighting bonfires.

Gambling was a popular activity in the southern colonies, even for children. People loved to bet money on horse races, cockfights, and wrestling matches. They also gambled on card games and dice games.

For the most part, Christmas was not heavily celebrated. Some colonists made merry by firing off guns, feasting, and attending church. The Puritans treated Christmas as just another day without celebrations. By the 1640s, Puritans fined people who wasted "precious time 26-27 in celebrating Christmas.

Members of the Anglican church celebrated Twelfth Night (January 6) more than they celebrated Christmas. Twelfth Night was the day when the Wise Men arrived in Bethlehem carrying gifts for the Christ child. On Twelfth Night, people gave presents, ate special cakes, and danced. Young couples often married on Twelfth Night.

Most often, colonists simply turned work into fun. Families invited neighbors to help gather a harvest, sheer sheep, or boil maple sugar. In return, the family provided plenty of food—and maybe music and dancing. "We invite a dozen neighbors," wrote one man, "who come . . . and finish [the work] in one day. At dinner we give them . . . pies, puddings, fowls, roasted and boiled. . . . Thus we help one another."

A crowded dinner in New Amsterdam. In 1664 the English took over New Amsterdam and renamed it New York.

❖ ❖ ❖ ❖

GAMES AND TOYS

Few games and toys in colonial days were created just for children. Portraits show children cuddling a pet or holding flowers or walking sticks. Toys are rarely shown. Toys purchased from a store were too expensive for a child's plaything. Fancy dolls, miniature tea sets, and dollhouses did exist, but they served as amusements for adults.

Often children made toys from simple things found around the house or outdoors. A blade of grass became a whistle. A milkweed pod held fleecy seeds that would dance on the wind. Girls made "babies" (dolls) from corn husks, hickory nuts, and rags, then dressed them in hand-sewn gowns. Boys prized their jackknives, tools for whittling a whistle or a wooden sword. They played leapfrog, marbles, and sing-song games such as "London Bridge Is Falling Down" and "Here We Go Round the Mulberry Bush." They frolicked with their pet dogs and cats and rode horses. In winter they strapped on ice skates or raced sleds down hills.

Colonial children were often expected to entertain themselves without the luxury of toys. Many enjoyed playing with pets.

Boys enjoyed more freedom than girls. They ran races and climbed trees or roamed the forests hunting and fishing. A girl wearing a heavy long dress and petticoats couldn't do those things. So girls found quiet pastimes. They practiced sewing neat and pretty stitches on "sampler" cloths. They read, played music, and practiced dance steps.

Colonial girls practiced sewing by making samplers (squares of cloth with many kinds of stitches).

PUBLICK TIMES IN WILLIAMSBURG

Williamsburg, the capital of Virginia, was lively during Publick Times. That was when government leaders got together. The whole town celebrated with a variety of entertainments. People crowded shoulder to shoulder on the village green (a central park) and marveled at traveling performers who put on puppet shows and Shakespearean plays. Audiences also loved fire-eating shows, magic, and card tricks. Some performers even demonstrated the latest scientific discoveries.

People of all ages played quoits (a ring-toss game), nine pins (a bowling game), and stool ball (a game where a ball was whacked around a course of wickets, or small gates). Young and old joined games of blindman's buff or hide-and-seek.

ABOVE SILLIER DIVERSIONS

Unlike their southern neighbors, colonists in New England shunned most amusements. Play was not encouraged after age seven. New England Puritans hoped to raise their children "above the sillier diversions of childhood." They did not want children to think "diversions to be a better and nobler thing than diligence [work]." Cotton Mather noted, "Recreations may be used now and then, but . . . let those recreations be used for sauce, not for meat." Toys only tempted children into idleness and make-believe.

> *"Recreations may be used now and then, but . . . let those recreations be used for sauce, not for meat."*
>
> —*Cotton Mather, a Puritan minister, 1690*

Still, New England children must have had their fun. Otherwise there would have been no need for a man to guard the boys' pew in church. Without the ever-present guard, the lads might have giggled together or carved the pews with their jackknives.

Cotton Mather's son Nathaniel recalled whittling on the Sabbath, which was forbidden. "For fear of being seen, I did it behind the door," he wrote. "A great reproach to God!" His poor father ached over how to lift the boy "above the debasing Meannesses of Play."

"To Improve My Dancing"

Colonists of all ages loved to dance. People pulled on their best clothes, then traveled miles to attend glittering dance parties called assemblies. Harpsichords (a keyboard instrument), lutes, and violins led dancers through lively French minuets and Scottish reels. As moonlight passed to morning sun, people danced, ate, and drank the hours away. "It was indeed beautiful," recalled one assembly guest, "to see such a number of young persons, set off by dress to the best advantage, moving easily to the sound of well-performed music."

Both boys and girls studied dancing. In March 1739, Mary Grafton wrote her father about dance lessons at her Philadelphia school. Mary hoped "to improve my Dancing" enough to "enable me to appear well in any Public Company." Some families hired private dancing masters to guide children through complicated dance steps. Books also offered dance instruction.

A poor dancer could be banished from future parties. In the

Dancing was not just for fun, it was a social requirement. Most colonial children, especially those from wealthy families, dressed in adult styles.

middle of one ball, a dancing master scolded a seventeen-year-old boy. The dancing master considered the fellow's manner "insolent and wanton." He threatened to dismiss the lad from further dance classes. Such embarrassment!

Early Puritans and Quakers forbade dancing. One Puritan minister in Massachusetts preached, "The Devil was the First Inventor of the . . . Dances." But even strict Puritans could not smother people's love of dancing. By the 1690s, the new royal governor of Massachusetts was hosting balls. Even churches found reasons to hold dances—such as welcoming a new minister.

CHAPTER SIX

GROWING PAINS

"At ten years old I was taken home to assist my father in his business."

—Benjamin Franklin, who quit school to work for his father at age ten, 1716

❋ ❋

By age twelve, most colonial children were preparing for their adult lives. By age sixteen, many youths shouldered grown-up responsibilities of jobs and marriage. Their childhood days were long over.

Many sons learned a trade by working alongside their fathers. A boy could learn blacksmithing, printing, and many other trades in this way. A son might also help run a family-owned business, such as a tavern or an apothecary (drugstore).

Some young men became apprentices (students of a trade). Many good careers began with apprenticeships. Apprentices gained skills as wig makers, silversmiths, and saddle makers. Even doctors and lawyers trained as apprentices.

Hat-maker.

Opposite: A young woman gathering apples. *Right*: An engraving of a hat maker and his apprentice

To become an apprentice, a boy and his parents signed papers binding over the boy to a master. The master promised to provide the boy with a home, food, and clothes as well as hands-on training. The apprentice promised to work long days cleaning, sweeping the shop, and running errands. He promised to stay away from taverns, theaters, and gambling places. He also pledged that he would not marry.

Boys usually became apprentices by age twelve. Some poor children became apprentices as young as age six. That way, their parents would not have to feed and care for them. Towns also saved money by apprenticing orphans at an early age. A young man's apprenticeship usually ended by age twenty-one. Then he entered adult life with the skills he had learned—and often a new set of tools.

An illustration of Ben Franklin working in his brother's printing shop in Boston

Girls also apprenticed. A girl could apprentice as a milliner (hat maker), dressmaker, cook, maid, or other job. A girl's apprenticeship usually lasted until she was seventeen or eighteen, or until she got married.

Ben Franklin worked for two years in his father's candle shop. "I dislik'd the Trade," he later wrote. So he apprenticed with his older brother, James. James owned a printing shop and published a newspaper, the *New-England Courant*. Ben learned to set tiny metal type, letter by letter, line by line. He worked the heavy printing press, edited news, and sold papers. He even wrote articles under pen names such as "Silence Dogwood."

In 1722 James was jailed for publishing articles criticizing the government. Sixteen-year-old Ben kept the paper going. At seventeen, Ben spread his wings, leaving Boston for Philadelphia. He had to sneak away. "If I attempted to go openly," he wrote, "Means would be used to prevent me."

In Philadelphia Ben got a job in a print shop and worked to "secure my credit and character as a tradesman." Trying to look as responsible as possible, he "dressed plainly" and "was seen at no places of idle diversion" such as taverns and cockfights.

* * * *

COLLEGE

America's first college opened outside Boston, Massachusetts, in 1636. The new school, founded by the Reverend John Harvard and named for him, was meant to educate ministers. Boys as young as twelve could attend Harvard. They studied grammar, writing, Latin, Greek, Hebrew, logic, math, and astronomy. Students roomed at the

A print of Harvard, 1739. College rules were strict, and sometimes student life was harsh. Harvard students rioted in 1766 over the stale bread served at meals.

college. They could pay their college costs with firewood and baskets of eggs as well as with money.

Some sons in wealthy families sailed for England to further their education at Oxford or Cambridge Universities. By the end of the colonial era, the colonies had nine homegrown colleges. But only a tiny percent of America's sons attended. No one dreamed that young women would ever attend.

* * * *

COME A COURTING

Marriage was an expected role for adulthood. In fact, a young woman's main job was to marry and raise a family. She was usually at least sixteen when she became a bride. A young man was usually twenty-one or older. At that age, he was able to support a family.

The notion that people might marry for love was a new idea during colonial times. For most couples in the middle or lower classes, the decision to marry belonged to them. Most often, young people met at dances, at church, or at a neighbor's

Marrying for love was a new idea in colonial times.

Wifely Qualities

house during a day of apple picking or barn raising. If a young man
was interested in a girl, he requested her father's permission to
"court" her. The courtship took place under the watchful eyes of the
young woman's family.

To wealthy parents, the marriage of a child was an economic
bargain. Their child could become richer or poorer, depending on
whom they married. Children raised in wealth had to ask their
fathers' blessing before marriage.

When two families agreed to a
match, both promised a dowry
(land and money) for the young
couple. Daniel Parke agreed to let
his daughter Frances marry the
son of John Custis in 1705, "if my
daughter likes him." Parke said he
would base his daughter's
"wedding portion" on the young man's belongings. As Parke wrote
to the elder Custis, "I will give her upon her marriage with him, half
as much as he is worth."

> *"I will give her upon
> her marriage with
> him, half as much
> as he is worth."*
>
> —Daniel Parke, speaking of his
> daughter's dowry, 1705

Never More to Meet

Sometimes upper-class parents thought a suitor was unsuitable. Then they might forbid their daughter to marry him. In a notice in the *Virginia Gazette* on August 2, 1756, one guardian reported that his niece, Sarah Homan, had eloped with a young man. The ad asked "all County-Court Clerks . . . not to grant them a Marriage License."

> *"To whom will you fly in your distress when all the world will upbraid [criticize] you with having acted an idiot?"*
>
> —Evelyn Byrd's father, 1698

Sixteen-year-old Evelyn Byrd's father forbade her from seeing the man she loved. In a furious letter, he commanded Evelyn "never more to meet, speak or write to that gentleman, or give him an opportunity to see, speak or write to you." If Evelyn married the young man, she'd get no money from her parents. And if Evelyn's love turned sour, her parents would not comfort her. "To whom will you fly in your distress," asked Mr. Byrd, "when all the world will upbraid [criticize] you with having acted an idiot?"

Evelyn Byrd obeyed. She broke off her friendship with this man. By her twentieth birthday, her father referred to her as an "antique." She died unwed before the age of thirty.

Unlike Evelyn Byrd, Judy Carter defied her parents and married "against her duty." For two years after her wedding, her furious father refused to see her. Judy's marriage was unhappy, and her father softened. He offered the "poor offending" girl some money "for personal necessaries." But he took care to "give nothing" that her husband could claim.

POSTING THE BANNS

Wedding ceremonies differed from place to place. They followed the traditions of the area and of the young couple's religion. Most weddings took place in church or at the bride's home. Wedding celebrations for rich and poor couples, in towns and on the frontier, usually included a special feast and sometimes music and dancing.

In Puritan New England, there were no ministers, wedding rings, or wedding clothes at weddings. Instead, a government clerk performed a simple ceremony.

Members of the Anglican religion "posted the banns" two weeks before a marriage ceremony. This public notice alerted people to the upcoming wedding so that anyone with a reason to stop it had time to come forward.

A wedding dance in the South

Quaker weddings took place with no minister or government clerk. Young people simply pledged themselves to one another in front of other Quakers at a Quaker meeting. After marrying, a woman's husband became her "lord." She owed him the same obedience she had given her father. In many homes, this was a loving relationship. One New England husband wrote that his wife was "subject to him, yet in a way of liberty, and not of bondage."

* * * *

LEAVING CHILDHOOD BEHIND

Children spent years struggling to grow up. They were drilled on rules on how to behave. They wrestled Death and the Devil. They prepared and trained for adulthood.

And what happened then? Sometimes children turned out lazy and wild. Some unruly teenagers got kicked out of the house by their parents. Some chose jobs their parents did not like. They married

In the mid-1700s, families enjoyed easier lives than the first colonists had.

people their parents did not approve of.

Most parents looked forward to the day a child married, began a career, and had children of their own. To have brought a child safely to adulthood was a proud accomplishment.

> "Youth is the time of getting, middle age of improving, and old age of spending."
> —Anne Bradstreet

Many people never reached old age. Those who reached their fiftieth birthday felt lucky to sit back, reflect, and enjoy. After all, from the days of the cradle, their lives had been filled with danger, hard work, and loss. As Anne Bradstreet wrote: "Youth is the time of getting, middle age of improving, and old age of spending."

ACTIVITIES

Study Historical Illustrations

Many illustrations showing colonial times were made later. Photography had not been invented. Artists did paint portraits, but only wealthy families could afford to hire a portrait artist. The illustration on page 41 shows George Washington in about 1750 (Washington was born in 1732). The illustration wasn't made until 1850, but it offers some well-researched clues about colonial life.

The two men with Washington are probably a gentleman and a slave. People in colonial America ranked people from high to low, like rungs on a ladder. Gentlemen and their families had the highest rank. People "of quality" came just below gentlemen in rank. Next (in order) were "those above the ordinary degree," the "better class" of people, "those of mean condition" (poor people), and servants. Last on the ladder were slaves. Most African American people were slaves.

Colonists dressed according to their place on the social ladder. Both Washington and the gentleman are well dressed. The gentleman is wearing a wig, a fashion of the wealthy. Both are riding fine horses. The slave is taking care of the hunting dogs. He is better dressed than if he worked in the gentleman's fields. Colonial children were raised to respect people in the ranks above their family. By sweeping off his hat, Washington is showing his respect. Washington isn't noticing the slave man.

Continue to ask questions as you look at some other illustrations in this book. When were they made? What are the people doing? How are they dressed? Make a list of clues about colonial life. Then compare your list with your life. Who do we look up to in modern times? Do we still have a "social ladder"? Think about it.

Behind the Taw Line

Many colonial children enjoyed playing marbles. To play, draw a circle about fifteen inches wide. (Colonial children usually drew a circle in the dirt, but you could also make one with masking tape on a floor.) Put some marbles in the circle. Make a line (called a taw line) about a foot away from the circle. Then, one at a time, each player kneels behind the taw line and shoots a slightly larger "shooter" marble at the other marbles, trying to knock them out of the circle. (To shoot the shooter marble, hold your palm up, curl your forefinger around the shooter marble, and flick it with your thumb.) Whoever knocks the most marbles out of the circle wins.

Eliza Lucas's Day

In 1742 Eliza Lucas (page 35) wrote a letter to a friend describing "Eliza Lucas's Day":

Wakes up at five o'clock in the morning. Reads educational books till 7:00. Walks in the gardens and fields to see that the servants are about their jobs. Eats breakfast. The hour after breakfast spent practicing music. Next hour spent studying subjects like French and shorthand. The time remaining before lunch is spent teaching her younger sister and two slave girls how to read. After lunch, Eliza spends another hour practicing music. Then she sews until "candle light." The evening is spent until bedtime in reading and writing letters.

Write a letter or diary entry about your day that a young person could read two hundred years in the future. Remember, your written words could become a primary source for future historians!

Play It Again, Johann

In the 1600s and 1700s, young people had no televisions, CDs, or computers. They did have live music. Many children learned to play instruments such as the flute, fiddle, or harpsichord. Even Puritans sang and played church hymns. Some famous European composers enjoyed by colonial Americans were Johann Sebastian Bach, George Frideric Handel, Antonio Vivaldi, and Wolfgang Mozart (who began composing music as a child). Visit <http://www.classicalarchives.com/index.html> to learn more about the hottest musicians of colonial times. Or check out some CDs from your local library and relax to the top hits from the 1750s.

SOURCE NOTES

7   Jeremiah Eames Rankin, "The Word of God to Leyden Came," in *An American Anthology*, Edmund Clarence Stedman, editor, *Great Books Online*, <http://www.bartleby.com/248/494.html> (n.d.).

7   William Bradford, *The History of Plymouth Plantation*, quoted in Roy Pearce, editor, *Colonial American Writing* (New York: Holt, Rinehart and Winston, Inc.), 46.

8   William Bradford, quoted in Alicia Crane Williams, "Women & Children First," *American History Illustrated*, November 1993, 47.

9   William Bradford, quoted in Pearce, 46.

12 Gottlieb Mittleberger, quoted in Noel Rae, editor, *Witnessing America: The Library of Congress Book of Firsthand Accounts of Life in America, 1600–1900* (New York: Penguin Reference, 1996), 31.

17 Elizabeth Saltonstall, quoted in Linda Pollock, *A Lasting Relationship: Parents and Children over Three Centuries* (Hanover, MA: University Press of New England, 1987), 207.

21 Benjamin Franklin, *Autobiography*, quoted in George McMichael, editor, *Anthology of American Literature: Colonial Times through Romantic* (New York: Macmillan Publishing Co., 1993), 340.

21 Alice Morse Earle, *Childlife in Colonial Days* (1899; reprint, Stockbridge, MA: Berkshire House Publishers, 1993), 308.

21 Cotton Mather, quoted in Pollock, 228.

22 Benjamin Franklin, quoted in McMichael, 340.

22 The Reverend John Robinson, quoted in John C. Miller, *The First Frontier: Life in Colonial America* (Boston, MA: University Press of America, 1986), 214.

22 Pollock, 210.

22 Miller, 61.

23 *The New-England Primer*, quoted in McMichael, 97.

23 Elizabeth Sprigs, "We Unfortunate English People Suffer Here," quoted at *History Matters*, American Social History Project, <http://www.historymatters.gmu.edu/d/5796/> (n.d.).

24 Isaac Watts, "Against Idleness and Mischief," quoted at *Selected Poetry of Isaac Watts (1674–1748)*, University of Toronto, <http://www.library.utoronto.ca/utel/rp/poems/watts2.html> (n.d.).

25 Rae, 62.

25 Cotton Mather, quoted in Pollock, 228.

26 Isaac Watts, quoted at University of Toronto website.

27 Samuel Sewall, quoted in Louis B. Wright, *Everyday Life in Colonial America* (New York: G. P. Putnam's Sons, 1972), 174.

28 Doctor Thomas Palmer, *The Admirable Secrets of Physick and Chyrurgery*, Thomas R. Forbes, editor (1690; reprint, New Haven, CT: Yale University Press, 1984), 81.

29 *The New-England Primer*, quoted in McMichael, 97.

29 Cotton Mather, quoted in McMichael, 202.

29 Samuel Sewall, quoted in *The Diary of Samuel Sewall*, Harvey Wish, editor (New York: G. P. Putnam's Sons, 1967), 65.

30 Increase Mather, quoted in Pollock, 109.

31 Anne Bradstreet, quoted in Pearce, 407.

31 Cotton Mather, quoted in Pollock, 125.

32 Joy Hakim, *From Colony to Country* (New York: Oxford University Press, 1993), 42.

33 *The New-England Primer*, quoted in McMichael, 96.

35 Anne Bradstreet, quoted in McMichael, 109.

35 John Winthrop, quoted in Rae, 54.

35 Maria Carter, quoted in Pollock, 137.

36 Betty Pratt, quoted in Julia Spruill, *Women's Life and Work in the Southern Colonies* (New York: W.W. Norton Co., 1972), 195.

36 Benjamin Franklin, quoted in Rae, 56.

37 Eliza Lucas, quoted in Ruth Moynihan, et al., editors, *Second to None: A Documentary History of American Women*, vol. I (Lincoln, NE: University of Nebraska Press, 1993), 134.

38 Miller, 233.

38 Mary Ball, quoted in Miller, 234.

38 Rae, 50.

39 Wright, 112.

39 Governor William Berkeley, quoted in Rae, 54.

39 Devereaux Jarrett, quoted in Miller, 111.

40 George Washington, *Rules of Civility and Decent Behavior in Company and Conversation* (1744;

reprint, Bedford, MA: Applewood Books, 1994).

41 William Fitzhugh, quoted in Miller, 219.

41 *The School of Manners* (1701), quoted in Rae, 62.

42 John Adams, quoted in Hakim, 63.

43 Francis Louis Michel, personal papers, circa 1702, William Hinke, translator, *Virginia Magazine of History and Biography*, April 1916, 114–115.

43 Wright, 207.

45 Hector St. John Crevecoeur, quoted in Victoria Sherow, *Huskings, Quiltings, and Barn Raisings* (New York: Walker and Co., 1992), 2.

47 Cotton Mather, quoted in Pollock, 228, 148.

47 Cotton Mather, quoted in John Warner, *Colonial America: Home Life* (New York: Franklin Watts, 1993), 98.

48 Nathaniel Mather, quoted in Wright, 216.

48 Cotton Mather, quoted in Miller, 212.

48 Phillip Fithian, quoted in Wright, 198.

48 Mary Grafton, quoted in Pollock, 231.

49 Phillip Fithian, quoted in Edmund S. Morgan, *Virginians at Home: Family Life in the Eighteenth Century* (Williamsburg, VA: The Colonial Williamsburg Foundation, 1991), 19.

49 Increase Mather, *An Arrow against Profane and Promiscuous Dancing Drawn out of the Quiver of the Scriptures* (1684), Home Page, Reformed Presbyterian Church (Covenanted), <http://www.covenanter.org/Imather/arrowagainstmixtdancing.htm> (n.d.).

51 Benjamin Franklin, quoted in McMichael, 340.

52 Ibid.

53 Benjamin Franklin, quoted in Wright, 64, 112.

55 Governor Jonathan Belcher quoted in Laurel Ulrich, *Good Wives: Image and Reality in the Lives of Women in Northern New England, 1650–1750* (New York: Alfred A. Knopf, 1982), 84–85.

55 Daniel Parke, quoted in Morgan, 34.

56 Morgan, 35.

56 William Byrd, quoted in Pollock, 271–272.

56 Landon Carter, quoted in Pollock, 274.

58 John Winthrop, quoted in Miller, 204.

59 Anne Bradstreet, quoted in Ernest Kohlmetz, editor, *The Study of American History*, vol. I (Guilford, CT: Dushkin Publishing Group, 1974), 132.

SELECTED BIBLIOGRAPHY

Calvert, Karin. *Children in the House: The Material Culture of Early Childhood, 1600-1900.* Boston, MA: Northeastern University Press, 1992.

McMichael, George, editor. *Anthology of American Literature: Colonial Times through Romantic.* New York: Macmillan Publishing Co., 1993.

Pearce, Roy H., editor. *Colonial American Writing.* New York: Holt, Rinehart and Winston, Inc., 1969.

Purvis, Thomas. *Colonial America to 1763: Almanacs of American Life.* New York: Facts on File, Inc., 1999.

Rae, Noel, editor. *Witnessing America: The Library of Congress Book of Firsthand Accounts of Life in America, 1600-1900.* New York: Penguin Reference, 1996.

Smith, Carter, editor. *Daily Life: A Source Book on Colonial America.* Brookfield, CT: Millbrook Press, 1991.

FURTHER READING & WEBSITES

Day, Nancy: *Your Travel Guide to Colonial America.* Minneapolis, MN: Runestone Press, 2001.

Fritz, Jean. *The Double Life of Pocahontas.* New York: Puffin Books, 1987.

Plimoth Plantation. *Plimoth-on-Web.* <http://www.plimoth.org>.

University of Missouri-Kansas City. *What Do We Know about the People on the Mayflower?* <http://www.umkc.edu/imc/mayflow.htm>.

Weidt, Maryann N. *Revolutionary Poet: A Story about Phillis Wheatley.* Minneapolis, MN: Carolrhoda Books Inc., 1997.

INDEX